'81

D1711934

All of these different animals are reptiles.

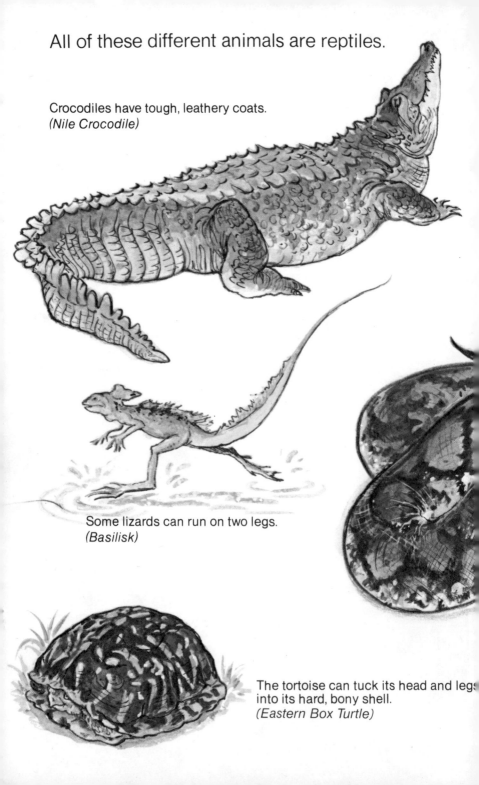

Crocodiles have tough, leathery coats.
(Nile Crocodile)

Some lizards can run on two legs.
(Basilisk)

The tortoise can tuck its head and legs
into its hard, bony shell.
(Eastern Box Turtle)

Some snakes and lizards can glide through the air as though they had wings.
(Flying Dragon)

This little thread snake is only six inches long.

This snake, at thirty feet, is the longest reptile.
(Reticulated Python)

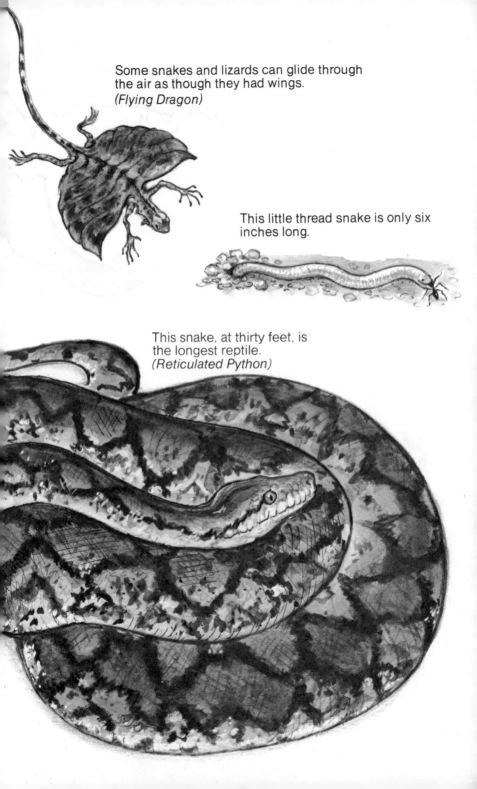

A Child's Book
of Snakes, Lizards,
and Other Reptiles

By Kathleen N. Daly

Illustrated by Lilian Obligado

Doubleday & Company, Inc., Garden City, New York

For Malcolm and Snakey

Library of Congress Cataloging in Publication Data Daly, Kathleen N.
A child's book of snakes, lizards, and other reptiles. Includes scientific
names. SUMMARY: An illustrated introduction for beginning readers
to reptiles including snakes, lizards, the tuatara, turtles, tortoises, and
crocodilians. 1. Reptiles—Juvenile literature. [1. Reptiles] I. Obligado,
Lilian II. Title. QL644.2.D34 598.1 Library of Congress Catalog Card
Number 77–16911 ISBN: 0-385-13584-X Trade ISBN: 0-385-13585-8
Prebound Text copyright © 1980 by Kathleen N. Daly Illustrations
copyright © 1980 by Lilian Obligado de Vajay All Rights Reserved
Printed in the United States of America First Edition

Contents

What Is a Reptile?

EVERYBODY knows what a bear or a bird or a fish is. But reptiles seem strange to most people. Frogs and toads are not reptiles. Neither are worms, eels, or salamanders.

Snakes and lizards, crocodiles and alligators, turtles and tortoises—all of these very different-looking creatures belong to the group of animals called "reptiles."

All reptiles are cold-blooded. This doesn't mean that their blood is cold. It means that their body heat changes with the temperature of the air around them. Many animals, such as birds and dogs and people, are warm-blooded. Their temperature remains pretty much the same whatever the weather outside. Reptiles have to move from place to place to look for a shady patch if they get too hot or bask in the sun if they get too cold. During the winter, or cool season, many reptiles simply find a sheltered place and doze off until the weather gets warm again. Most reptiles are found in places where the weather is warm all year long.

Another thing that reptiles have in common is that most of them lay eggs. The eggs are a little like birds' eggs, except that their leathery shells grow into lumpy shapes as the babies inside get bigger. Most reptiles don't look after their eggs and hatchlings the way birds do. The mothers lay their eggs, cover them over, and go away.

Reptiles breathe air, just as we do. Even a sea snake or a marine turtle must come up to breathe, though not as often as we do when we swim.

All reptiles have scaly skins, though the skin of a snake or a lizard may seem smooth, while that of an alligator is tough and leathery and the turtle's back is a hard shell.

Reptiles come in many different sizes and shapes and colors. Some of them may look quite startling. Some you can hardly see. All are well suited to blend with their backgrounds—mud brown or leaf green or shadow-speckled.

Once upon a time, long ago, long before there were any people on earth, there were hundreds of huge scaly reptiles, the biggest creatures that have ever lived on earth. They were the dinosaurs. You can see some of their huge bones at a museum. You will notice how much they look like the lizards, turtles, snakes, and crocodiles alive today.

Lizards

NEARLY all lizards have four legs and can run about very quickly. Sometimes they even run on their two back legs. Their long tails help them to keep their balance. Most people enjoy watching lizards that seem cheerful and lively. But many lizards sit still for long minutes at a time and seem hardly to breathe.

Their skins are dry and scaly and usually smooth and neat looking. But others have crested backs, ruffs around their necks, or untidy-looking spines all over their bodies. Their colors may be green or brown or gray. They may be spotted. They may change from one color to another in a few minutes. Some have sacs under their chins that they blow up like tiny balloons.

Many lizards are quite at home in the water. The plumed basilisk can even skim along the top of the water on its long toes. Other lizards can dive, often from high up in trees near a river or lake.

Plumed basilisk running on water.

Some lizards live in burrows under the ground. The Florida worm lizard, blind and pink, is one of these. It is hard to tell its head from its tail!

Others live in tree branches and hardly ever come down to the ground.

Some live in holes among rocks or in stone walls.

Florida worm lizard.

This frilled lizard
has its collar up.

The flying dragon.

The African chameleon catches insects with its long tongue.

It clings onto a branch with its toes and tail.

Its eyes can swivel in different directions.

The friendliest and most useful lizards live in people's houses, where they eat up insects.

Like most reptiles, baby lizards hatch from eggs. They are able to take care of themselves as soon as they are born.

They keep growing all their lives, until they die. (Most other animals stop growing at a certain age, when they become "adult.") Sometimes you may see a lizard with untidy, whitish bits of stuff hanging from parts of its body. This is its old skin, which it is shedding in bits and pieces. Underneath is a beautiful new skin. Lizards (and snakes) keep on shedding old skins all through their lives as they keep growing bigger.

If you try to catch certain kinds of lizards by

A lizard's tail breaks off easily.

the tail, they may run off, leaving a bit of tail behind them! The tails of many lizards snap off very easily. New tails grow back in their place.

Instead of running away from danger, a lizard may turn and stare at its enemy, bouncing up and down and doing tiny pushups, trying to look very fierce. Lizards have many ways of protecting themselves.

Even a large dog can be frightened off by the sight of an Australian frilled lizard raising its umbrellalike cape and opening its pink mouth.

The flying dragon of Asia has flaps alongside its body that allow it to glide from branch to branch. When the flaps are folded, the little creature looks like a small insect.

The common chameleon is one of the most remarkable lizards. It stays very still in the branches of a tree, waiting for an insect to come by. Slowly the color of its skin changes so that it looks like the color of the tree. The insect does not see the chameleon and may come quite near. Then suddenly out flicks the chameleon's long, sticky tongue to catch the insect. The chameleon coils the tongue back into its mouth, swallows the insect, then quietly waits for the next one to come along. It can keep a sharp lookout all around it

A male anole with its neck and throat inflated.

Marine iguanas are much larger than their land cousins.

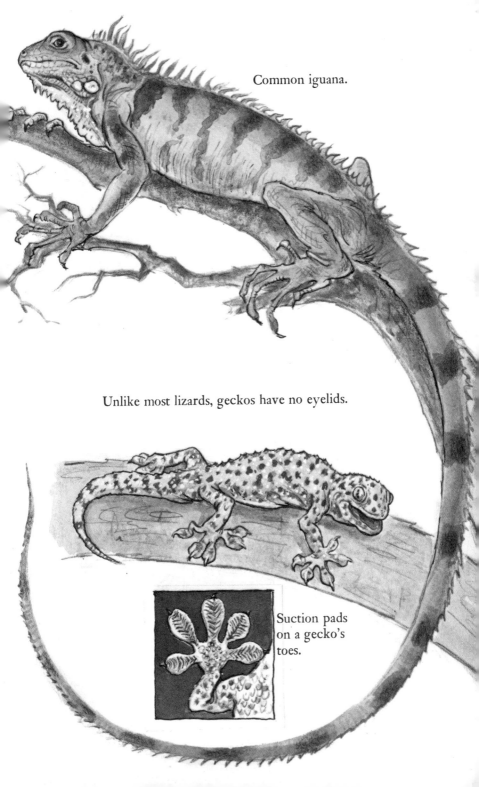

Common iguana.

Unlike most lizards, geckos have no eyelids.

Suction pads on a gecko's toes.

without moving its head, for each eye can swivel independently in every direction. Its curling toes and long tail keep it still and steady.

The anole is often called the American chameleon because it, too, can change its color to match its surroundings. It is much livelier than its African cousin. It is usually bright green with a pinkish or yellowish throat that it puffs out to show off.

The common iguana is the big lizard found in tropical America. It is grayish green, with a crest that runs down its back and tail. With its large eyes and down-turned mouth, it looks a little sad.

The large marine iguana is one of the few lizards that feeds in salt water. It lives in the Galapagos Islands in the Pacific. It eats seaweed from the rocks and catches insects. Hundreds of marine iguanas bask together on the rocks, making a carpet, one spiky tail on top of another.

Geckos are among the few reptiles with voices. These friendly creatures often live like pets in houses in hot countries. They chirrup to each other as soon as the sun goes down. You can imitate the sound by clicking your tongue against the roof of your mouth and silently saying, "Gecko." Try it!

The six-lined racerunner is a silky-skinned lizard that you may see in Florida or the Caribbean Islands. It darts about in yards among chickens and children, leaving sandy places covered with its slashlike tracks.

Horned "toads" of the Southwest are really lizards. They have an amazing collection of spikes, warts, and flaps of skin all over their bodies. They look very much like molochs, which come from Australia but are not related.

Only two lizards in the world are poisonous. They are the Gila monster of the American Southwest and the Mexican beaded lizard. They look like brightly colored beaded bags. They live in the desert and are very shy.

The Komodo dragon of Indonesia is a monitor lizard, the largest of all lizards. Some are ten feet long. It chases small animals and can knock them over with a lash of its long, strong tail.

The six-lined racerunner is fast and lively.

The horned toad may squirt blood from its eyes to frighten away enemies.

The Gila monster grows up to two feet long.

Stay away from the Komodo
dragon, little pig!

Snakes

SNAKES are related to lizards, but there are no snakes with legs. One of the wonders of snakes is that even without legs they can move about so fast and in so many places.

There are sea snakes, "flying" snakes, burrowing snakes, snakes that climb trees, and snakes that slither, streak, or "sidewind" across the ground.

Flat, belly scales help a snake move across almost any kind of ground except slippery glass.

The belly scales of a snake.   The hinged jawbones of a snake.

There are many strange things about snakes. Snakes never blink—true, because they have no eyelids. They even sleep with their eyes open. The unblinking stare frightens many animals and people.

Some people think snakes are cruel and cunning. Not true! Snakes have small brains and are not very intelligent. They kill their victims quickly. They have to, for they have no arms or legs to fight with, and their skin and bones are delicate. Their hinged jawbones open wide to swallow an animal whole, and their backward-slanting teeth prevent the animal from escaping.

The bulge in its middle tells us that this snake has just swallowed a small animal. The snake won't eat again for many days.

The slender emerald tree boa is an agile tree climber.

The anaconda is sometimes
called the water boa. It hunts
for food in the water.

The boa constrictor is ten
to twelve feet long.

Many people think all snakes are poisonous. This is not so. Their forked tongues are only used for "smelling" the air. Most snakes kill by squeezing or "constricting" their prey.

Like lizards, snakes shed their old skins as they grow bigger. If you are lucky enough to find a whole snake skin, you will see that it even includes the snake's eye coverings. Underneath the old skin the snake has a brand-new coat, often brightly colored and patterned with spots, stripes, and diamond shapes.

Pythons and boas, which live in the tropics, are the biggest snakes. They are not poisonous. They are constrictors, which means that they will kill their prey by squeezing.

The reticulated python is the biggest of all snakes and may grow thirty feet long. A mother python is one of the few snakes who coils around her eggs until they hatch.

The anaconda, a boa, is almost as big as the reticulated python. It lives in trees and in swampy riverbeds in South America. Its eggs are hatched inside the mother. About seventy young wrigglers are born live and ready to take care of themselves.

The snake has no more use for his old skin.

The boa constrictor is another large snake, with handsome markings. Though it can easily kill big animals, it can also be tamed as a pet. It will coil around a person in a friendly way, enjoying the warmth of a human arm or neck.

The emerald tree boa is easy to recognize. When it is resting it coils itself neatly over a branch, with its head resting right in the middle of the coils. As a youngster, before it gets its beautiful green color, it is yellowish or brownish, rather like a bunch of bananas on a branch.

A mother anaconda with her young.

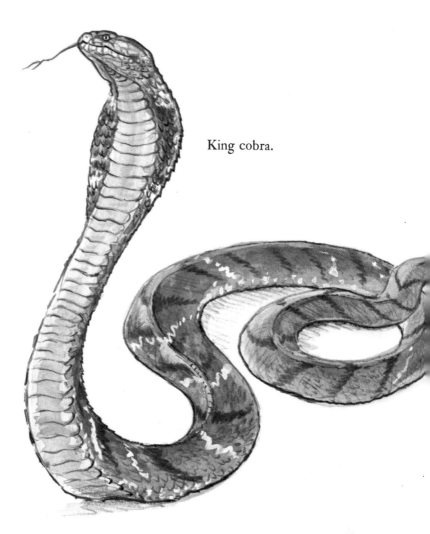

King cobra.

This hog-nosed snake is playing dead.

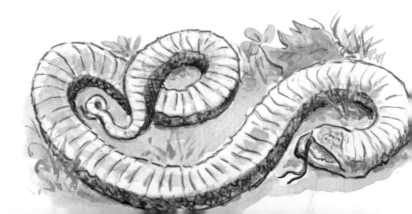

Indian or spectacled cobra.

The rubber boa can roll into a ball.

San Francisco garter snake.

The rubber boa is a small snake, only eighteen inches long. Its head and tail look very much alike. When attacked, it curls into a ball and raises its tail as if it were a head. Very puzzling for its enemies!

One of the commonest snakes in North America is the garter snake, of which there are many kinds. They are usually striped, but may be spotted, and in shades of yellow, black, green, and brown.

The East Indian flying snake can climb up smooth, steep surfaces. It can glide, or "fly," from one tree to another by spreading the skin over its ribs and taking a leap.

A flying snake actually glides.

The small, two-foot-long, hog-nosed snake of North America is well known as an actor. When it is attacked, it puts on a very good show of being badly hurt, writhing about and then lying quite still and playing dead. After this act, its enemies usually walk away to look for a "live" snake.

Egg-eating snakes of Africa, of which there are many, eat eggs by opening their jaws wide to take them in, piercing them with sharp spikes in their throats, then spitting out the eggshells.

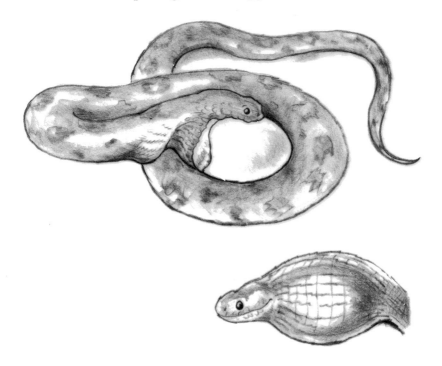

A snake swallows an egg.

Western diamondback rattlesnake.

Sidewinder.

Coral snake.

Cottonmouth.

The king of the poisonous snakes is the king cobra of Southeast Asia. It may be more than fourteen feet long. Some people say it is the most intelligent snake. It is the only snake that makes a nest for its eggs. Both father and mother cobras stay nearby until the babies are hatched. In zoos, king cobras learn to know their keepers and their feeding times. When it is angry, the king cobra flares out a hood around its neck to scare its enemies.

Many cobras, including the Indian or spectacled cobra, have impressive neck hoods.

One of the prettiest poisonous snakes is the coral snake of the Americas, banded in red, black, and yellow. Some similarly banded snakes are not poisonous, and it is very difficult to tell the difference between them.

The cottonmouth or water moccasin is a pit viper. It doesn't live in a pit! It has a small pit, or hollow, in its skull, that helps it to feel the heat of an animal nearby. When alarmed, it opens its mouth wide, showing an inside white as cotton. The cottonmouth is poisonous.

The rattlesnake is native to North America. Like all snakes, it sheds its skin as it gets bigger, but this one adds another scale at the end of its tail each time it molts. When the snake is agitated it "rattles" its tail. The loud noise may scare its enemies away. The diamondback rattlesnakes are beautifully marked. Their bite is poisonous.

New tail "buttons" on a young rattlesnake.

The sidewinder is a rattlesnake that moves in a "sidewinding" way, leaving a J-shaped mark as its trail.

The Tuatara

THE TUATARA looks like a lizard, but scientists have discovered that its peculiar skull bones make it different from any other animal on earth. They call it a "living fossil," for it is the one and only creature that has remained unchanged since even before the days of the dinosaurs, many millions of years ago. There is only one kind of tuatara. It lives only on some tiny islands off the coast of New Zealand.

The tuatara is very slow moving. It may not even breathe for over an hour! It shares burrows with sea birds such as petrels. It comes out to hunt at night when its bird roommates are asleep.

It is one of the few reptiles with a voice and croaks mournfully, like a lonely frog.

The tuatara.

Turtles and Tortoises

MOVING "as slowly as a tortoise" is moving very slowly indeed. But never mind. The tortoise has been around for a very long time and it lives to a ripe old age in almost every subarctic climate.

The turtle carries its armor-plated "house" on its back. The picture shows what a turtle, or tortoise, looks like inside. Its top shell is a carapace, its bottom shell a plastron. The land tortoise can pull its head, tail, and legs into its shells and be safe from a bear's paws or a person's knife or almost anything.

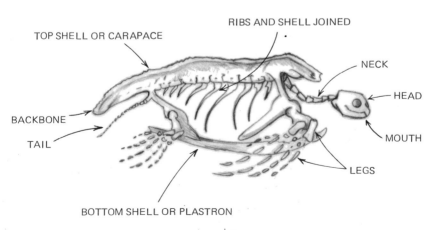

Cross section of a turtle.   33

The Galapagos tortoise is the largest land turtle. It can weigh as much as 500 pounds.

The seagoing leatherback is the biggest of all turtles. It is about eight feet long and weighs 1,500 pounds or more.

Another giant of the sea is the hawksbill turtle. Its scales overlap like shingles on a roof.

Turtles live on land or in the sea or in freshwater ponds.

They can weigh as much as 1,500 pounds. Or they can be small enough to fit into the palm of your hand.

Sea turtles, such as the giant leatherback and the hawksbill, have legs that look like flippers. They can swim very fast, but most often they are seen flapping slowly along like huge underwater birds.

Whether they live on land or in water, turtles must come ashore to lay their eggs. It is very difficult for a sea turtle to lumber ashore and dig a hole with her flippers. Often she does this at night, by the light of the moon. After the eggs are laid, she covers up the nest and goes back to the sea. When the babies hatch, they, too, find their way to the sea.

Not all turtles have the same kind of shell. Some are hard and scaly and ridged, some are smooth. Some are so soft-shelled that the turtle can slip into a narrow crack between the rocks and inflate itself to keep out enemies.

The box turtle is probably the commonest land tortoise in North America. Like most tortoises it can withdraw completely into its shell and shut up tight—unless it gets too fat! Pet turtles often eat too much and get lazy. When they try to hide in their shells, an arm or a leg may stick out because there just isn't room enough under the shell for the fat little body.

If you keep a pet turtle, it is important to learn just how, what, and when to feed it, so it will live for a long time.

You may see a diamondback terrapin poking its head out of the waters of tidal shallows and streams. It needs salt water to live.

Stay away from the snapping turtle! Although no turtles have teeth and are usually gentle and shy, the snapper can give a nasty bite with its horny beak and strong jaws.

The alligator snapping turtle catches fish by wiggling the tip of its tongue. To a fish, the tongue looks just like a tasty worm and the fish ends up in the turtle's jaws.

Painted turtles are common almost everywhere. You'll know them by the yellow and red stripes down their heads and necks.

Small musk and mud turtles may give off a strong smell when scared. Sometimes they are called "stinkpots" or "stinkjims."

Common or eastern box turtle.

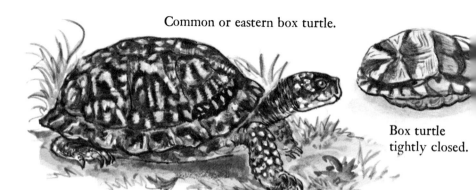

Box turtle
tightly closed.

The soft-shelled turtle has a long, skinny neck.

The musk turtle is one of the smallest turtles in
North America (about four inches long).

The gopher tortoise digs itself underneath the desert
sand to shelter from the sun.

The diamondback terrapin often hangs in the water with only its
head showing.

This alligator snapping turtle is about to catch a fish for dinner.

Crocodilians

ARE CROCODILES the monsters that ancient people used to call "dragons"? They don't spout flames and smoke from their nostrils, but they are certainly fierce and dangerous creatures.

Like many other reptiles which live in hot countries, crocodiles and alligators spend their time near water. They eat fish, water birds, eggs, or any animal, including an occasional person, that comes too near their huge jaws.

Crocodiles have long bodies and tails, and bellies covered with tough armor plating. Their long snouts are full of teeth. Their nose openings are on the tip of the snout, and the eyes are high up on the head. A crocodile can cruise around under water with nearly all of its body hidden but can still breathe and see very well.

When it swims, the crocodile tucks up its legs close to the body and propels itself with its strong tail.

A basking crocodile often keeps its mouth open for extra cooling. Sometimes birds come and pick its teeth.

The crocodile welcomes its tooth-cleaning friend.

The American alligator and the Nile crocodile look and act very much alike. Both have teeth that hang untidily down from the upper jaw. Only the crocodile has a tooth that sticks *upward* from the lower jaw.

Both of them are good mothers, which is unusual for reptiles. The alligator builds a nest of mud and leaves, while the crocodile digs a hole in the sand or makes a burrow in a river bank.

When the eggs are laid (from thirty to sixty eggs), the mother covers up the nest and waits nearby for about ninety days.

The American alligator mother stays close to her nest.

The gavial has a long, tooth-filled snout.

The Nile crocodile mother carries her young in her mouth.

When the young are ready to hatch, they squeak from inside their eggs. The mother answers at once, for she must help the hatchlings out of their enclosed nest.

Once the babies are free of their eggs, the mother carries them gently in her mouth to the water. She may stand around for several days or weeks, while the youngsters bask on her back or on nearby logs, learning the ways of the river or lake and croaking to each other like frogs.

Angry crocodiles and alligators, both male and female, ROAR! Their bellows can be heard for miles around.

Alligators make "gator holes" by swiping at soft sand and mud with their tails as they bask in the sun. The hollows then fill up with water and make handy swimming ponds for small alligators.

The American alligator has a much smaller cousin, the Chinese alligator, only four feet long.

The caiman of South America has a snout like the alligator, with tucked-in teeth.

The jacare, also of South America, is called "spectacled" because the bony ridge between its eyes looks like the bridge piece on eyeglasses.

The gavial (or gharial) of southern Asia is a small creature with an extremely long, narrow snout. The snout is filled with dozens of sharp teeth, even in size, and very useful for catching fish. Like all the crocodile family, it uses its teeth for seizing and holding, not for chewing.

All crocodiles and alligators live in fresh or brackish water except for one—the saltwater, or estuarine, crocodile. This one prefers seacoasts and river mouths (estuaries). Sometimes it takes to the ocean. It has been seen thousands of miles from land.

When we speak of "crocodile tears," we mean make-believe tears. The crocodile does shed tears, but only to get rid of too much salt and to clear its eyes of sand. And all the while, it seems to be smiling a wicked smile.

Scientific Names of the Reptiles in This Book

THERE are thousands of different kinds of reptiles in the world. Some look and act very much alike, while others seem entirely different from one another. You'd never confuse a lizard with a turtle, for instance, but it might be hard to tell a marine iguana from a common iguana. To make things easier, scientists, using Latin, the universal language of science, have given every reptile its own special *species* name. To show how it is related to certain other similar reptiles, it has a *genus* name as well. For example, the snake we know as the western diamondback rattlesnake belongs to the group, or genus, of snakes known as *Crotalus*. In that group, its special name is *atrox*. Its full scientific name is *Crotalus atrox*.

The *genus* and *species* of each of the reptiles in this book are listed below, in the order in which they are illustrated in the text.

About the Author

KATHLEEN N. DALY was born in London, England. She spent her childhood on the island of Mauritius (in the Indian Ocean) and in France and Scotland. Ms. Daly has been a children's book editor in both England and America and is the author of more than forty books for children, many of them on the plants and animals of the world. She now lives in New York City, with a charming boa constrictor.

About the Artist

LILIAN OBLIGADO was born and grew up in Argentina, on a ranch where she had many small wild animals as pets, as well as numerous cats, dogs, and horses. Ms. Obligado came to the United States, where she has illustrated many children's books. She and her husband and two children now live in Paris.

All of these different animals are reptiles.

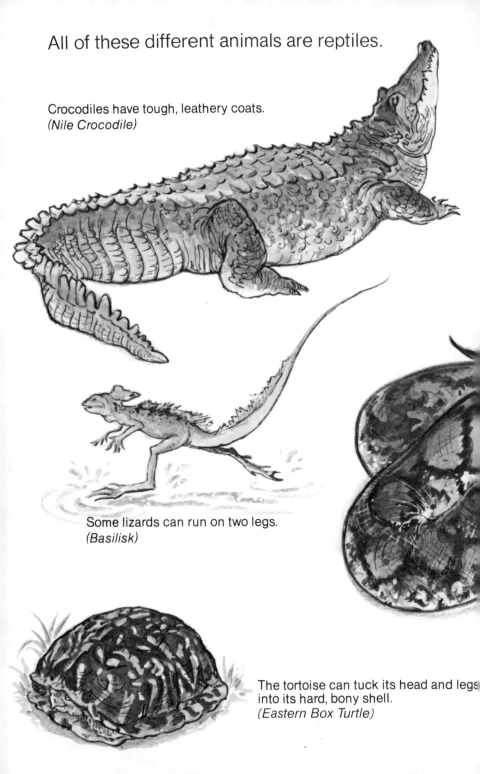

Crocodiles have tough, leathery coats.
(Nile Crocodile)

Some lizards can run on two legs.
(Basilisk)

The tortoise can tuck its head and legs
into its hard, bony shell.
(Eastern Box Turtle)

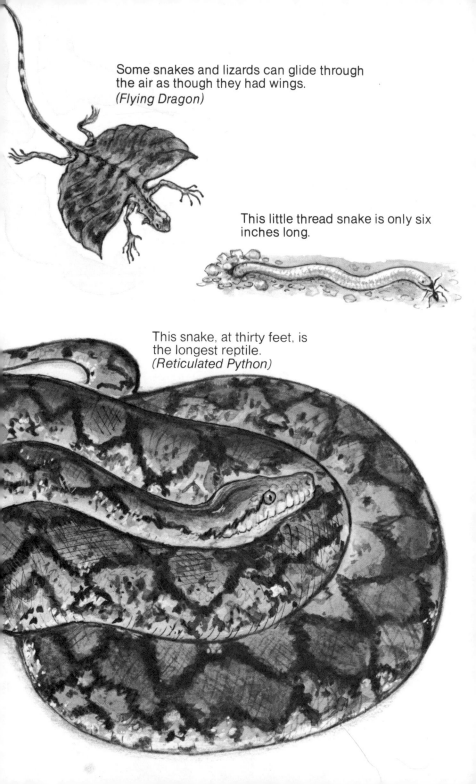

Some snakes and lizards can glide through the air as though they had wings.
(Flying Dragon)

This little thread snake is only six inches long.

This snake, at thirty feet, is the longest reptile.
(Reticulated Python)

DATE DUE	
APR 26	
JAN 2 7 2004	
MAR 1 2 2004	
APR 3 0 2004	
SEP 2 8 2004	
OCT 1 1 2004	
MAY 3 2005	
MAR 1 4 2007	
APR 4 - 2007	
NOV 8 2007	